Silent Music
Adam Wyeth

salmonpoetry

Published in 2011 by
Salmon Poetry
Cliffs of Moher, County Clare, Ireland
Website: www.salmonpoetry.com
Email: info@salmonpoetry.com

ISBN 978-1-907056-65-9

Typesetting & cover design: *Siobhán Hutson*
Cover artwork: © *Ronfromyork* | *Dreamstime.com*

Salmon Poetry receives financial assistance from
the Arts Council / An Chomhairle Ealaoin

For Mike and Paula

Acknowledgements

A number of these poems have appeared before in various magazines, journals and anthologies. 'Google Earth' was commended by the Arvon International Poetry Competition, 2006, and published in their 25th anniversary anthology. 'Leland Bardwell,' 'Dad,' 'Chamber Music', 'Carry The Torture', 'Cinema Complex', '*Deoch An Dorais*', 'Rough Music' and 'Ode to The Globe' were published in *Agenda* (UK). 'Life is Shit' was published in *Poetry London* (UK). 'Hell' was published in the anthology *Something Beginning with P*, (O'Brien Press, Ireland). 'Silent Music', 'Alfa Romeo Giulietta Spider Veloce' and 'Night Train' were published in *Southword* (Cork). 'A Viking Comes to Tea' was published in *Magma* magazine (London). 'Those Were The Days' was published in *The Stinging Fly* (Dublin). 'Idagy' and 'Blackout' appeared in *The SHOp* (West Cork). 'The Long Run' was a prizewinner in the Fish International Poetry Competition, 2009, and was published in their anthology. 'Google Earth', 'Oxbow Lake' and 'A Viking Comes to Tea' were published in *Landing Places* anthology, 2010 (Dedalus Press). 'Pinter's Pause' was published in *Southword*'s online journal. 'Google Earth' and 'Oxbow Lake' also appear on the Poetry International Web. 'Life is Shit' and 'A Viking Comes To Tea' are kept in the Southbank Centre's online library. 'Google Earth' and 'Silent Music' were read on RTE radio and C103fm.

Thanks also to all the people who have helped me with my work over the years: including Paula McGlinchey, Mike Godden, Desmond O'Grady, Matthew Geden, Afric McGlinchey, Ian Wild, Greg O'Donoghue, Pat Cotter (and the old Thursday workshop team), Derek Mahon, James Harpur, Gerry Murphy, Matthew Sweeney, Susan McKeown, Joe Sweeney (and the new team at the Bishopstown Tuesday workshop), Patricia McCarthy, Maurice Riordan, Thomas McCarthy and Elaine Feeney.

"The best music in the world is the music of what happens."

FINN MCCOOL

Contents

Google Earth

The poet's eye, in fine frenzy rolling,
doth glance from heaven to earth, from earth to heaven.

Theseus from *A Midsummer Night's Dream,*
Act V Scene I

We started in Africa, the world at our fingertips,
dropped in on your house in Zimbabwe; threading
our way north out of Harare into the suburbs,
magnifying the streets – *the forms of things unknown,*
till we spotted your mum's white Mercedes parked
in the driveway; seeming – *more strange than true,*
the three of us huddled round a monitor in Streatham,
you pointed out the swimming pool and stables.
We whizzed out, looking down on our blue planet,
then like gods – zoomed in towards Ireland –
taking the road west from Cork to Kinsale,
following the Bandon river through Innishannon,
turning off and leapfrogging over farms
to find our home framed in fields of barley;
enlarged the display to see our sycamore's leaves
waving back. Then with the touch of a button,
we were smack bang in Central London,
tracing our footsteps earlier in the day, walking
the wobbly bridge between St Paul's and Tate Modern;
the London Eye staring majestically over the Thames.
South through Brixton into Streatham –
one sees more devils than vast hell can hold –
the blank expressions of millions of roofs gazing
squarely up at us, while we made our way down
the avenue, as if we were trying to sneak up
on ourselves; till there we were right outside the door:
the lunatic, the lover and the poet – peeping through
the computer screen like a window to our souls.

Plane

I'm trying to capture the small plane
as it snores through the siesta of each afternoon;
the whole of county Cork rolls out like a scroll
to our house near the sea on the edge of the plane.

He climbs the causeway of clouds and nearly turns
into a full stop beyond the squiggly lines of cirrus,
then coming back towards us, switches
off his engine and glides freehand with the terns.

I find him here on my sky-patch, flying solo
most days, as I'm hooked over my writing pad
catching the rays; he hovers overhead like a bee
drunk on too much pollen – sometimes so low

I can make out a face. We're on the same page
I imagine, as he waves down to me in the garden,
wondering what I'm writing before he lifts the nib
of his nose and buzzes behind the bushes – off the page.

-Winged-Hope-

I wonder how you are in your humble abode,
in the Bungalow, Belvedere, Blackness road?
The alliteration raises my heart's alarm –
as if it belongs in an Emily Dickinson poem,

oppresses, like the Heft of Cathedral Tunes.
I'm reading her bittersweet verse,
and find you skulking between the lines,
hiding from friends behind blinds –

or the shield of a half-open door.
I think of you *before you got your*
eye put out: a carefree girl with Audrey Hepburn
flair – a tan to match – legs 11 –

working in the bank where you met dad.
What happened then? – I'll never know –
how you were dragged into the shadows
to unravel *your bandaged soul.*

My stiff Heart questions was it He –
who sent you into the House of Cold?
Or was it responsibility as the eldest child
living in a large household?

Dickinson knew what it was like to hide,
known as the Myth of Amherst –
never leaving her childhood home
till the day she died.

All I can do is wish you *-winged-hope-*
that you will fly once more
like the words in her poems
– flanked with dashes – to help them soar.

Rough Music

The whole village came out to clamour
and clash, a constant crescendo
of pots and pans outside his house –
like somebody crashing down the stairs.

Ransacking cupboards, emptying cutlery
drawers in a calamity of noise.
One neighbour took his wooden spoon
and whipped up a storm in a beer mug,

while women played merry hell,
smashing saucepan lids like cymbals,
dragging their claws down washboards.
Droves of men hauled necklaces of tin cans

along the road and marched to the beat
of buckets being battered out of shape
with crowbars. Innovative, like some kind of
travelling circus playing the antithesis

of a Romeolovestruckyouth – serenading
on his lute below a balcony window.
Upstairs the culprit was lying curled up
in bed, as though he'd been kicked in the guts

seeing stars like the ones his wife saw
the night he punched her in the jaw.

Exit Music

(i.m. Mike)

How apt it was. The moment we raised
your coffin a jazz band started to play; sending
you off in the jingle-jangles of New Orleans echoes.
Not spluttering or stalling in solemn procession

like the clapped out *Citroen* you once bought
without your hearing aid – and thought
was silent as a *Rolls*. They sprang into gear
full of sparks and flight, blowing trumpets

and trombones as if life depended on it,
all pistons firing like your brand new 1920s *Bentley*.
I saw you again, decked out in goggles and scarf,
dashing over hills and dales –

dazzling each passer-by, before roaring off
in a trail of dust.

Chimanimani Mountains, Zimbabwe

(for Paula)

Some day she will go back to her home
of the quartz crystal mountains.
She will slip through the gateway –

and see her past rolled out
like some old map of mythical places –
knowing each contour as her own cartography.

She will stumble upon familiar faces –
sons and daughters of those she knew.
The mountains will be her shadow,

following her wherever she goes.
Under a yawning acacia – she will fall
asleep – as sweet balsamic scents

fill the valley's breast. Stirred
at dawn by cries of the crested eagle –
she will join her ancestors again –

moving hypnotized like a tribal dancer –
rumbling over the hills with drums of thunder,
carried by the wind.

Special Place

It's not the palatial gardens of the Taj Mahal,
or the lakes and mountains of Donegal;
nor is it that paradise beach flung out at sea
listening to the gentle swell under a palm tree.

For me, it's back in the heart of Sussex
where you and I pick out the white exotic
flesh of steamed langoustine from their pink shells;
eye-level with rhododendrons and bog asphodels

dipping their toes in the shade of the stream;
listening to your flamboyant expositions on dreams,
while tractors in the field peel strips
of gold and fold them like pastry into giant nuggets.

From behind my ear, you pluck a love-in-a-mist
and begin to unfold each petal like a horologist
taking apart its multi-layered design,
then put it back together. Every time.

Oxbow Lake

From Lesotho to Sullivan's Quay,
Maurice Scully inscribed in his book
of poetry to me. Because I caught
wind of him mentioning a Basotho blanket
in one of his poems. We got
talking – how we both went to Lesotho:
seeking adventure, growing our hair.
And we ran through places
we visited there, like a river snaking down
the mountains, till our paths
criss-crossed here – converging
like an oxbow lake. From The Kingdom in the Sky
to the People's Republic of Cork
below the sea. And under his signature
X marked the spot to me.

X marked the spot to me
below the sea, and under his signature,
to the People's Republic of Cork.
Like an oxbow lake from The Kingdom in the Sky,
criss-crossed here – converging
the mountains. Till our paths
we visited there, like a river snaking down.
And we ran through places,
seeking adventure, growing our hair.
Talking – how we both went to Lesotho
in one of his poems. We got
wind of him mentioning a Basotho blanket
of poetry to me. Because I caught
Maurice Scully – inscribed in his book,
From Lesotho to Sullivan's Quay.

Alfa Romeo Giulietta Spider Veloce

I see you in my mind's eye driving your Alfa,
your *Alfa Romeo Giulietta Spider Veloce*.
Never happier, winding through country
lanes of Devonshire; darting over the moors.
Taking to the road as Vikings took to sea
in search of plunder. No wonder
at eighty-five you drive a sky-blue Mx5
convertible, you call Malcolm,

collecting me at Tunbridge Wells station,
tearing home to catch the last of the sun –
puffing on your Peterson's I bought
in Dublin, our smiles and words
briefly catching each other,
before taking wing on the wind.

Dad

I'll always remember those Sunday drives home.
How a blackening silence came over us
with the night. I'd look back at the road
we'd set out on when our weekend had begun:

singing songs, stopping at petrol stations
in the back of beyond, turning off the beaten
track and finding a pub for lunch –
with swings and climbing frames to play on.

But all that was fading fast, as signs marked
the dwindling miles, oncoming headlights
dazzled us, the final catseyes blinked past
and the road emptied – losing its nerve

as we curved off the motorway. Then the real
darkness set in – the chill of parting
making me numb. I'd run upstairs to my room
without a word spoken, and from the corner

of my window watch your silver *Citroen* slip
into the night; a final sliver of light then total eclipse.
Another week of staring into space in classrooms,
waiting for our next outing all together. Save mum.

Starry Nights

Drawing the curtains
I let them in,
each pinprick of light
stabbing the night –

a macro-map of synapse knobs
switching on and off,
bringing to mind
Vincent Van Gogh

opening a window
on his subconscious,
splashing the heavens
on to countless canvases;

his bleary eyes twinkling
under a flickering
candle fixed to his cap –
an explorer poring over a map.

Looking back in time,
he believed each gob and swirl
of light was the soul
of dead poets.

Till one black night,
drinking absinthe to absent friends,
he spotted himself
on a dotted line

of constellations –
and had to laugh,
firing the firmaments
with his autograph.

★ (to be read from the bottom-up)

for the first time.
like seeing a lover undress
as the land was revealed fresh,
and know something of Adam
with our ancestors
to touch fingers
pull back His black mantle –
is to see the hand of God
Some say to witness the break of day
with blue and ochre pastels.
suffusing the sky
rising from the horizon –
with the lid rattling off,
like a simmering pot
clouds seep out
as it crowns over the hills;
before the sun
night bends over backwards
down on one knee,
the globe tilts on its axis –
to the back of the mind
dreams disperse
where last night's ghosts reside;
creeps into woods
like steam from fields
Mist lifts

Sunrise★

Waiting for the Miracle at Ballinspittle Grotto

Nothing moves but cars.
First one passes, then I see
a second coming.

Leland Bardwell,

night I could not sleep
I came to read you in lamplight –
poking from the rushes
of books festooned on my shelves
that I look upon as family.
But Leland, you were the least familiar
of kith and kin, given me
by your son, Nicholas, in Dingle.
And so, Leland Bardwell,
I opened your pages like arms
and undressed you.
My eyes, my ears, my nose, my hands,
my mouth – watering inside –
devoured you! Night I could not sleep,
Leland Bardwell,
I came to you out of the rushes of sheets,
and held your slender spine
tenderly as the first time I found poetry
singing in me.
The lines of your life on Lower Leeson Street
opened and closed like windows
in my mind, and the sun and moon rose
at the same time.
Leland Bardwell, night I could not sleep
I came to raise the dead
weight of my head from its rushes of knots
and lay it on your lap
where your lyrics ran like fingers through my locks.
Night cannot contain
the strain of thoughts that fly between these walls –
so I have come
to settle them in words
plucking them
from the air, from where all things come.
Such thoughts
I had while reading you, Leland Bardwell,
night I could not sleep.

Carry the Torture

Today I must remember
to email my father,
who has a tumour
the size of a cucumber
growing in his liver.

It came like a whisper
by text from my sister.
She says he's in good humour
but I'm sure he'd rather
not suffer chemo all summer.

Truth is, he's known all winter,
felt it growing bigger,
tried to keep it under,
till it jutted from his figure
like the Dingle peninsula.

Only then did he call the doctor.
My dad, who thinks he's bigger
than life – who never bothers
to lift his finger and dial my number,
who told me not to whimper

when I was a wee nipper,
who gave me the cold shoulder,
is now looking for a shoulder
to cry on. I could raise my finger,
but now I've grown older,

I no longer carry the torture.
It's him that's grown bitter,
and like a witch doctor
has taken the disorder
down into his liver –

spreading like a rumour.

Finding Rumi

Despite the threat of an imminent attack
I'm inwardly calm, enjoying the warm
breeze on my cheeks as it drifts up
from Saudi Arabia; sipping apple tea

with my semi-automatic on my knee,
while watching my leader deliver a speech
on TV. He looks different today, more
like my Uncle Said, still, we all look alike

to the West; that's what my brother in London
tells me. He's been rubbing shoulders with MPs,
says things are *oil well!* over there. He writes
punned headlines for a tabloid paper.

Once, I would have torn him to shreds,
but then I found a book of poetry by the great
Sufi mystic Jelaluddin Rumi. Years of hostility
peeled away like an onion; I was freed.

Now I am dust particles in sunlight,
the musical air coming through a flute,
I'm a dervish – whirling under the sun
with no shoes on. Beneath this biohazard suit.

Chamber Music

The one piece of music that churns my stomach
is Schubert's Quintet in C

since my grandmother told me
this is what Nazi officers played full volume

to drown out the moans of millions of Jews
as they were led into those rooms.

No matter how stirring a pitch the violins reach,
or how plangently the rasping cellos sigh,

I see their gaunt naked forms fall like flies
in a poisonous fog, reduced to cow pat

lining the floors, then shit-shovelled into pits –
while the whole movement plays over and again

never reaching the end, like a scratched record
that keeps jumping back

like a ghost.
hovering over your head
from the cherry bowl –
one long tail would spiral
dreaming something up,
when you were
Some nights in the stillness
I'd follow as you spoke.
each trail of grey matter
across the room in smoke,
Puffing your ideas
drifting towards the ceiling.
a silver sibilance
with a wave of your hand,
then parting the smoke
a disappearing act behind smog –
with the glow of your pipe,
You lit up the night

Up in Smoke *

A Viking Comes to Tea

He didn't knock, rammed through the door, ranting
and raving in old Norse. Sniffed about the place –
then, gathering pieces of debris, proceeded
to make a fire in the middle of the room.
I had cream and jam scones all prepared,
but knew he'd be happier gnawing on the dog's bone.
He didn't speak much, what with the language
barrier; mostly murmurs and grunts, belches
whilst chewing, and bellows before he downed
in one – the pot of tea. When it rived
his throat and insides I thought his horns
would really show, but *au contraire* –
after his face went scarlet and he roared
like thunder, pummelling his belly like a drum,
he became strangely calm.
And beneath the forest of oleaginous whiskers
I detected a faint smile. He began stroking
my hair and feeling the fabric of my dress.
So I took him upstairs and showed him
my garments. He loved bright colours
but most of all he loved the softness.
I brushed out his plaits, shaved his beard
and ran a hot bath. I prepared dinner:
moules mariniere, followed by sauté chicken,
ending with crème brulee. He looked like a princess
as he came down in my wedding dress.
I showed him how to eat delicately.
Then after coffee – listening to Wagner –
the beast in *me* guided his hand.

Butterfly Daughter

Each morning before school
she prises herself from her cocoon,
a wood nymph – from the depth
of the earth – transforming in her room:

the painted lady, marbled white,
meadow-brown, orange-tip,
hairstreak, every pattern and hue,
then takes off into the Adonis blue –

her peacock wings opening –
weighed down by a festoon of bling.
A new person each day she leaves –
a clouded yellow heart on her sleeve.

Pinter's Pause

(for Paula)

It was the height of summer.
We sat in the garden reading a play.
I played him and you played her.
Before long you said, 'Do you know about
Pinter's pause? – those silent moments –
pregnant with words unsaid...'

I wasn't really listening, I thought I saw
a fox in the undergrowth –
stopping by the hedge to eye up his purple gloves.
Everything was in flower.
We read the play right the way through.
I was him, she was you.

Looking up during each pause –
I imagined him creeping beyond our garden
wriggling under the gap in the fence
behind the clematis and convolvulus –
or whatever it was? The twist of hedgerow,
the turn in the lane, the height of the day.

Just then, everything stopped,
caught between the hands of a clock.
The sun was at its zenith;
I thought if I put my hand out,
I could catch it and put it in my pocket.
I didn't want to say anything, to break the spell.

Then it moved on –
like a great cog in a grandfather clock.
The season was passing,
our lives were turning before its eyes.
Those soft paws padding the undergrowth,
gingerly treading between the hedgerows –
beyond the clematis and convolvulus

The House in the Woods

(for Mike's friends at Sweethaws)

after Kipling

They bulldozed the house in the woods,
all that remains is a gap in the trees –
a black patch of roots, scrubland
and brambles where the front room used to be.
The bay window has closed its eye
over the pond for good.
If anyone came they wouldn't know
there was once a house in the woods.

Yet if you visit this place on a summer night
when the last light shines on the silver birch
and fingers of fern unfurl
from the cooling earth
fanning perfume of bluebells and thyme –
you might hear in the conifer leaves
spirited conversations,
in the cheeps of finches
the chinking of glasses –
and conveyed on the slightest breeze
a commanding voice
telling tales as tall as the trees;
as if you knew this old house in the woods...
But there is no house in the woods.

A Million Tanks in Cork

When I first heard it, collecting
my change, I imagined an army
of truculent, armoured vehicles
elbowing down Carey's Lane,

flattening passers-by like an end-
is-nigh, apocalyptic movie. The image
blew up like a city fire in my mind.
Perhaps it was an Irish curse,

an innate aversion to my right angled
accent buffeting against the soft curves
of their rain-washed burrs.
Till I noticed everyone shooting

the breeze with it for the smallest
exchange: a loaf of bread, a bottle of wine,
each one passing it on like the Eucharist
or a virus that had got out of hand;

then saw it for what it was: a fusillade
of gratitude, an inquisition of appreciation,
the machine gun fire of obligation
charging in every direction.

Night Train

(for Greg O'Donoghue)

A Guru once said:
when somebody dies
you should feel happy
to make the passing
of their spirit easy.

So though the day is dark
we keep our spirits up
with whiskey – talking
about the best of times.
And we all wear smiles,

plastered to our faces
like clowns. Hoping
and waiting –
like a family outside
a maternity ward –

for the delivery of a baby
falling soft into the lap
of this world. Except
we hope for a safe
departure,

that all lines are open,
so you can cruise,
quiet and smooth
as a night train –
through invisible planes.

The Revolution of Breath

I was listening to Allen Ginsberg on the air
talk about Bob Dylan.

Watching him from the wings, Ginsberg said,
Dylan had become identical to his breath –

as if a shaman conjuring all of his consciousness –
like a shaft of light, a column of breath.

And I thought of Maharishi, who died yesterday,
the last days of his life spent in seclusion –

not wanting to waste his breath; he sat in
meditation waiting for the last mouthful of air

to leave his body, and at the point of death
became a single breath.

Life is Shit

my brother said over the phone.
After thirty-odd years of being alive
this was his assessment of it.
I concurred, taking a moment to digest it...

which took me back to when we were kids,
sent to our room for being little shits.
Bored, we took an empty biscuit tin
from under the bed; my brother squatted,

dumped in it. I did the same, then inspected it,
our first science lesson: dissecting it
with Lego bits, finding nuts and chocolate chips,
taking it in our hands and playing with it

like funny clay or Christmas cake. Then –
the inevitable, my brother being the eldest,
dared me to try a bit – all mixed up now,
not knowing which was which,

I took a bite: *how does it taste?*
my brother's grin filled his face.
I was too young to know the Old English
term from Chaucer's day – but if I did I'd say,

like shit! Just then it hit the fan,
mum came in and saw my face covered in it.
Chocolate spread? No! My lips painted thickly
like a clown. Now we were really in it.

Much older, I'd almost forgotten –
but some mornings after the daily ritual
I get up – and before sending it down the pan,
across our hometown, through the river,

under the bridge where we played Pooh sticks –
I take a look at it and I'm reminded.
Apparently it's good to do it –
my doctor said you can tell what shape

you are in by the shape of it: long and firm
is what you want; small lumps or runny bits
you have to watch your diet. Which helped me
find something encouraging to tell my brother

over the phone. 'Yes,' I said. 'Life is shit –
but sometimes it's good to look at it.'

Sycamore

I have moved my desk
to the window – so I can see
the sycamore again. I like to watch it.
Perfect specimen of a tree: upright, noble,
an almost total circle; a giant brain towering
over – not cowering down like a weeping willow.
Its million tipped branches grow up in orderly steps,
reach out like fingers. Soon buds will burst into leaf,
wrapping the tree within a globe of green. Brand new,
they will conceal any suggestion of fall for a hundred
days or more; spreading a shawl in total abandon,
forgetting their roots: the naked truth of winter,
when everything's stripped bare, holding on
till the bitter end. Now
it seems to beg
my stare, leaning
its muscular bough
toward the window,
stock-still as a voyeur.
Who knows what it's
thinking, whether those
tentacle tips aren't
picking my brain as well?

Telepathy

they put them in the bubbles now.
That's the champagne you exclaim –
I hear bells!
the closer together the better.
like champagne bubbles ourselves,
We bob
and we're growing up.
and down is close to the ground
left or right, only up and down
how there's no black and white
I borrow a phrase from Dylan –
are millions of hidden universes.
beyond our senses
Life's a bubble you say –
we rise for every toast.
The fizz goes to our head,
bottoms up!
raising our spirits,
tickling our noses,
out of glasses,
jumping like sprites
Bubbles climb to the top
flutes ringing like bells.
we raise them to you:
You fill our glasses –
and off our heads.
ricochet round the room
hit the ceiling –
Corks pop,

Bubbly *

Deoch an Dorais

Those winter nights
I became familiar
with their ways –
all touch-and-go
not a soul, save mine –
prodding a peat fire.
Then, winding down
they'd all trundle in –
fishermen out of the deep
like warriors from battle
sinking pint after pint
of dark ruby stout.
By two-o-clock
they were still drinking
whole-heartedly,
speaking in tongues,
my hands were tied
for who was I –
a tongue-tied blow-in
to show them the door,
to call *deoch an dorais* –
one for the road –
as if I were one of them?
Little did they know
my fathers too
fought for this land –
they assumed
by my muted tones
I was pure Sassenach
and after eight hundred years
to keep a sock in it.
Little did they know.
When the fire got low
I stood by the door
and watched them go.

Ode to the Globe

Wandering to the bottom of the garden
to cut off the artichokes, you return
with other worlds in your hands.
If they're not picked soon

a finely-haired flower sprouts out the top:
resplendent as fox gloves, you say.
A steady steaming for forty minutes
and we're away, plucking off

each soft frond, spading them
in melted garlic-butter –
then scraping the flesh off the saturated leaf
with our front teeth. The leaves getting thinner,

allowing our minds to drift,
till there's no flesh left on the inner tips.
Discovering the best of both worlds –
like Buddhists journeying towards

the centre of the mind, peeling back layers
to reach new realms. And though we sit
in calm repose, letting clouds of thought
come and go at our ease,

it's this we've been waiting for;
we pull off the yellow tufts of hairs
to reveal the round, concaved gem
and eat the heart out.

Hell

It was hot as hell
that summer, so just for the hell
of it I ran away. Like mum, I traversed hell's
half acre and created hell.
I thought, dad won't have a cat in hell's
chance of catching me, come hell
or high water I'll escape. But hell
for leather he found me. Hell's
bells, he yelled. What the hell's
your game? There'll be hell
to pay for you until hell
freezes over! And he did give me complete hell.
But he'd been so hell-
ish to mum I kept my hell-
acious self up. I was hell-
bent in galling him, so to play hell
I pulled out his beloved hell-
eborine as soon as we got home. Of course all hell
broke loose. He said I was just like my hell-
cat mother, but I know he still loved her hell-
enic beauty deep down. Since she had left we had gone to hell
in a hand basket, he turned home into a total hell-
hole. I missed mum like hell,
thus I became the hell-
ion I was, descending rapidly on a hell-
ward course. There wasn't a hope in hell
for me. I didn't say hell-
o to anybody anymore. I became hell-
raiser as much as possible. Then like a bat out of hell
I absconded again, with some Hell's
Angels this time; we had a hell-
uva ride. Dad thought I was definitely in for hell-
fire, and I did go to hell
and back over everything. But I wasn't a real hell-
hound. Just like any rebel, I was confused as hell.

DOWN
SLOW
on the tip of its black tongue a warning to
SLIPPERY WHEN WET
every notice revealing a lyric:
to the highway of the stars;
lighting up the banks like a runway
of whitethorn and gorse
lead back in time to a hedgerow
Signposts pointing the wrong way
in the middle of nowhere.
scuttling off to die
like a wounded animal
then coming to an end
a fairy ring road
or branching off
over a new leaf
each bend turning
like Celtic knots
going round in circles
through ancient riddles of hills
their blarney boreens twist and snail
Irish roads tell a different tale
and their high-speed highways.
emblematic of America
he scribbled *On the Road*
of tracing paper
one hundred and twenty-foot scroll
like Jack Kerouac's
in my rear view mirror,
and fall beneath in an endless scrawl
would rise to meet me
I'd make it so each line
If I was to write a poem on the road

May the Road Rise *

Wannabe Poet

I want to wake in a war,
have my home ransacked,
and family shot;

flee the country,
plot a revolution;
become a famous bullfighter...

then arrested for sleeping
with numerous men;
defend not only myself,

but all humanity; say
the ancient Greeks celebrated
males sporting their limbs

in gymnasiums, while judges
tied white ribbons
round their desirables;

because I want to be
thrown into gaol,
spat on and half-starved.

After I'm released,
coughing blood, I'll go to a tavern,
get stabbed –

then stagger downriver
scribble a quick note, and drown...
my body, unfound.

The Long Run

Run! Like you've never run before!
Hurtle past the turtles on main street,
bear left at the station – go straight
through the lights – and leg it like a March hare
past Biddy's bar – God rest her soul.
Run you langer run!
Run like you mean it – like you want it,
run like a herd of Elephants are chasing you,
run and find out!
Run through the evening into the red sunset –
melting on the end of the road like a pill on your tongue,
run like you own the whole macadam, run
and run into next week running into next month.
Smack your feet along the wet jowls of the rough road
like a passionate lover – *the course of true love*
never did run smooth. Run and don't look back,
don't hesitate, don't wait for the devil at the crossroads –
just keep flinging one foot in front of the other –
bolt blindly on like the Charge of the Light Brigade,
you're halfway there, think of me cheering you on –
shouting, run you fecker run!
Run over the Galtee mountains,
run through the rambling boreens of Tipp –
run around the dark edge of Europe –
run past the famine and diaspora,
run through the uprising and the burning houses –
run through The Republic and Troubled North.
Keep going, hang a right at the EU –
race the Celtic Tiger to the 21st century,
then run on like the gingerbread man –
sprinting past the ballot box of the Nice referendum
and the Lisbon Trick or Treaty –
run till you have no soles – run your socks off,
run bare foot if you have to –

one last leg and you can see the finishing line –
you're nearly there –
go hell for leather to the Cliffs of Moher –
Now jump you daft eegit – *jump!*
In the long run we are all dead.

Blackout

After the dust settled
and the rubble had gone
the sirens were dismantled

and our husbands came home;
we no longer had the excuse
to roam the streets at night

and rendezvous, catching
each other's eyes in the light
of bombed out buildings –

as we did during the blitz.
You'd put your coat
round my bare shoulders

and we'd suck down
your last cigarette.
Fags are always nicer shared.

Your whispering breath tickling
my ear, your red lipstick coating the butt.
The rush and blush of the city on fire,

echoed my heart, thumping
like a bomb about to go off.
At first, I thought it was only us,

but then I noticed others;
hearing muffled moans
behind cloaked windows.

On nights when you never came
I'd wander alone amid the blaze
trying to find you in alleys

we had known – the black curtains
flapping out of windows, like ghosts;
blowing me out like a flame.

Lord of the Mountain

(Hundreds of children currently work in the unsafe mines
of Bolivia. Eight million people are said to have died there)

We live between worlds
of darkness and light

in the mountain
that eats boys alive,

hang crucifixes
at the mouth of the fiend;

entering – a stone silence.
Light turns black,

lowered into the underworld,
out of Jesus' jurisdiction –

no looking back.
We pray for Satan's protection

our own resurrection
from this burning Inferno.

We call him *Tio* –
Lord of the Mountain,

deliver us from what we know.
Outside, people dance

in a carnival of colour
while we become shadows.

So many disappear
beyond the torch's flicker –

under the tunnel vision
of *Tio*'s glare.

The stories I've heard
I'm afraid to echo,

in case they rise like the dust
that stirs in our lungs –

swallowing us –
into the belly of limbo.

Oink

How many times
have I been to market?
Let me count the ways
on your tiny toes:
with dirt on my face,
my clothes a disgrace.
Houses of blowaway
straw and sticks – until
unyielding bricks. Some
live well on my back,
but most bring me home
straight from the poke
all sliced and wrapped –
only good when I'm sizzling.
They think I'm dirty, greedy,
that something's lacking.
But kids enjoy my wash of Latin.
Churchill was fond of me
and the police are named with me.
I'm the one who got up
and slowly walked away.
All animals are equal, but
(purse your lips)
some are more equal than others.
Keep telling porkies about me
and one day I might fly
all the way home.

Idagy

We spoke it all day. No one could understand us.
We shared secrets: who we fancied or disliked.
Gurgling our words, giggling about people
at lunch break. Back in class you said how

Mrs. Watson's nose looked like church bells –
her nostrils flaring in unison as they rang.
Her thick specs, I said, magnified her
God-fearing eyes like stained glass windows.

Thus we continued. But after school
Mrs. Watson kept us behind and yelled,
Idagy heardagurd whadagot youdagoo saidagaid!
Translated: we were dead.

Whirligig

(for James, Charlotte and Jon)

When buying it
in a flat package
I wondered how
the slivers of wood
attached only
by one central pin
became the graceful,
three-dimensional ornament.

Twisting each segment
into a staircase formation,
it took shape.
I hung it by the window
and there was Life!
Suspended serpentine,
a double helix.

Spinning it, I watched ripples
and spirals dance –
soaring helium balloons.
Slowly, winding to a halt,
dewdrops fell –
waves moving in and out
like children's laughter –
whirligiggling themselves
again and again.
Unravelling the genetic code.

Silent Music

People paid money to watch
someone seat himself
by a grand piano
without playing a single note.

The musician, as if in deep meditation,
didn't even lift the piano lid.
Then after nearly twenty minutes
he got up and left.

But somebody else
had already done the same thing.
Thus he sued this composer
for plagiarising his piece of silence

and won the case.
So as I sit here this evening –
the light low and everything quiet –
I listen to the silence

that plays all around me
in my room, wondering
if I've heard this piece before –
and who it belongs to.

Seeing Naples

Remember our sojourn to Naples? –
we nearly perished on those crazy streets.
Life is on the road in Napoli –
the alfresco hectivities of a million souls...

and in between skirts Death, buzzing on
one of those waspy vespas, sending black plumes
of smoke in his wake. Losing ourselves
in a labyrinth of lanes, gobbled up

by stupendous buildings fallen into disrepair;
colours clashing like Neapolitan ice cream:
medieval churches, tumbledown palaces –
rubbing shoulders with lords and whores.

Remember stumbling upon the *Pio Monte
della Miseriacordia* along a back alley? –
it housed Caravaggio's masterpiece,
The Seven Acts of Mercy.

It looked like an everyday *Napoli* scene –
a photo we'd taken off the streets.
Washing hanging like giant prayer flags
from every balcony, people rushing and shouting

like damned spirits of the underworld;
non compos mentis. Napoli, non basta una vita!
City of unfading imagination, where gods merge
with mortals – as rubbish putrefies the streets.

Famous Danish Poets

Over Danish pastries and tea,
I asked my wife do you know of any
famous Danish poets? She said no
I do not know of any famous Danish poets.

I said do you know why you do not
know of any famous Danish poets?
She said no I do not know why I do not
know of any famous Danish poets.

So I took a line from a Robbie Burns
poem: *O my luve's like a red, red rose;*
and regurgitated in Danish: *my luve's like*:
A ROUERR, ROUERR BLOMSTER!

Sounds like someone throwing up, said my wife.
That is why there are no famous Danish poets.

Cinema Complex

The weekend dad didn't come
mum announced we were going out;

she flung her jacket on and we sped off
to the cinema complex –

I had never been just with her;
sitting in the back row

I longed to touch her.
We watched *Back To The Future*

and *I* was Michael J Fox –
going back in time to save his parents.

He had to make sure they kissed
to the slow number at the dance

otherwise they would never fall in love
and he would never be born.

But he was getting to know his mum
all over. She was innocent, radiant

before she'd met his father.
Fox could have had her

if he wanted. He could have
warned her, while brushing his lips

against her unexplored ear,
to turn her back on the future.

Apples

I arrived crunching on the crisp flesh
of golden delicious, at break I tucked
into the juicy red ones. For the rest
of the week I spent all my lunch money
on them. By Friday I was famous
and feeling a little dizzy in class.

For the first time the tall girl caught my eye,
her cheeks flushed as she handed me
a selection of apple-scented hand cream,
bubble bath and shampoo – the girl
who usually had her hair in a bun
was now letting her soft curls fall
all over her school uniform –
and smelling sweeter than apples.

the end of the line!
as my head reaches
a resurrection –
a single exclamation,
taut as a tightrope,
fizzing esses onto the air,
my forked tongue
an up-and-coming Houdini,
by my escapology,
hypnotized
hundreds of eyes
a little more comfortable –
slipping into something
shedding my skin –
a transcendental meditation,
my kundalini spine –
uncurling
to Prince Charming –
climbing the poison ivy
like a lovelorn teenager
of the rising scales –
hanging on each note
up the spiral staircase –
a strange force sending me
I take to the air –
under his spell
turns me on;
till a winding horn
Wrapped up in myself,

Snake Charm *

King of Siam

I'm forever leaving my umbrella
behind like a bad memory. My gift
from you, or rather the thing you
threw as I walked out. Sometimes
I think it is a harbinger of my
misfortune, after all I only need it
when the heavens open; and round
here it's regular or is it regularly
irregular? It always comes back,
secure in the hands of a considerate
stranger – like a boomerang –
instant karma. At times I want to say
you can have it, as if I am a king of Siam
giving a white elephant for a present.

Guru Dave

He was telling us how he died years ago –
as if talking of another person. Now we try
to get our tongues round his spiritual title:
Premanand – a Sanskrit word. After his rebirth

he took to dressing in robes, buried his face
inside a beard – like a cloud – meditating
on a mountain in India, joined an ashram,
didn't come down till his old name and visa expired.

But beneath the disguise and swami one-liners
we see the ghost of the man – and behind his back
we still say *David*, or *Guru Dave* for a giggle;
sometimes we slip and say it in front of him –

to which he loses his mystic cool and snaps: *Premanand*,
the name's Premanand, PRAY – MAN – AND...

Those Were the Days

when nothing changed
and winters dragged on
chimneys choked
snow inched towards doors
piled at windows
and though the land
looked soft
as if smothered
under eiderdown
each day was a pillow
held over our faces
nothing grew
except long icicles
above the windows
like stalactites
we broke off
and licked like lollipops
our only hope
the wireless
not even crystal voices
of reporters
could take our minds
off this ice age
as we chewed
our chapped lips
waiting for the weather
like beggars
hoping to get some change

Robin

(for Mike)

Blood-bright, upright,
stopped, a red light;
its tiny black eyes the size
of pips on a dice.

Every day he comes
like a messenger,
taking me back to the verandah
where you charmed the birds

out of the trees. You had him
eating from your hand,
trained him to peck nuts
you held between your teeth.

This is love, you told me.
Legend says, the robin mopped
the cuts from Christ's head,
staining its breast blood-red.

Now I imagine you,
whistling back from beyond:
your ruddy-tuft chest
all puffed on your twiggy claws,

twitching your delicate beak.
I evoke my own folklore,
where I lure you in
with a palm of seeds...

The Door

I sit in the garden
taking the late sun
as it sinks and slides
between the side
of the house
and the hawthorn.
Trailing the bench
across the lawn
to catch a final
finger of warmth,
a golden stretch
comes to rest
on a patch
of grass at my feet
– like a door.
A door in which
I wait for your
shadow to darken;
the door, which is
always left open.

(27th March 2010)

About the Author

ADAM WYETH was born in Sussex in 1978, and has lived in Co. Cork for ten years. He was a prizewinner of The Fish International Poetry Competition, 2009; and commended by The Arvon International Poetry Competition, 2006. His poems have appeared in several anthologies including, *The Best of Irish Poetry 2010*, *Dogs Singing: A Tribute Anthology* (2010), *Landing Places* (2010), *The Arvon 25th Anniversary Anthology* (2006), and *Something Beginning with P* (2004).

Photo: Stefan Syrowatka

His work has appeared in numerous literary journals, including *The Stinging Fly, The SHOp, Southword, Poetry London* and *Magma*. He was a featured poet in *Agenda*, 2008 and 2010, and selected for the *Poetry Ireland* Introductions Series, 2007. He is also a featured poet on the Poetry International Web. He has made two films on poetry, *A Life in the Day of Desmond O'Grady*, first screened at The Cork Film Festival, 2004; and a full length feature, *Soundeye: Cork International Poetry Festival*, 2005. Wyeth is a member of the Poetry Ireland Writers in Schools Scheme and runs an ongoing online Creative Writing workshop: www.creativewritingink.ie. He is also a freelance journalist with a regular column at *The Southern Star* and is a book reviewer at the *Irish Times. Silent Music* is his first collection of poetry.